LIFE STORY

ELEPHANT

SARAH BLAKEMAN

Illustrated by
James Field

Troll Associates

Library of Congress Cataloging-in-Publication Data

Blakeman, Sarah, (date)
    Elephant / by Sarah Blakeman ; illustrated by James Field.
        p.   cm. — (Life story)
      Summary: Describes the physical characteristics, habitat, and
    behavior of African and Asian elephants.
        ISBN 0-8167-2769-4 (lib. bdg.)   ISBN 0-8167-2770-8 (pbk.)
        1. Elephants—Juvenile literature. [1. Elephants.] I. Field,
    James, 1959-   ill. II. Title. III. Series.
    QL737.P98B52   1994
    599.6'1 — dc20   91-44728

Published by Troll Associates

© 1994 Eagle Books

Design by James Marks
Edited by Kate Woodhouse
Picture research by Jan Croot

Printed in U.S.A.

10 9 8 7 6 5 4 3 2 1

Photographs by:
NHPA/Peter Johnson: 19, 29
NHPA/Peter Pickford: 11, 25
NHPA/S. Robinson: 23
Survival Anglia/Jen and
    Des Bartlett: 7, 15, 17, 21
Survival Anglia/Bruce Davidson:
    cover, 5
ZEFA/Aiken: 13
ZEFA/Damm: 27
ZEFA/G. Dimijion: 9

INTRODUCTION

A big, gray animal with massive legs, large ears, and a long trunk. What is it? Of course—it's an elephant! Two million years ago it could have been one of the many mammals with trunks, including the mighty mammoth. Now only African and Asian elephants survive.

African elephants are the largest land animals in the world. Adult males can weigh up to 12,000 pounds (5,400 kilograms)—about the same weight as 6 cars. They live in the bush and forests of Africa. This book will help you find out more about these magnificent animals and the way they live.

Elephants usually live in family groups of eight to ten animals, although some herds are larger. Sometimes, several family groups join to form bigger herds. All the adults in families are related females—mothers, daughters, sisters, aunts, and nieces—but some of the young ones may be males. Females are called cows, and males are known as bulls. The leader of the group is a cow called the matriarch. She is usually the oldest and biggest animal.

4

The family members depend on and help one another in times of need, such as when a baby elephant is born.

The birth of a baby is an exciting event for the elephant family. After nearly two years developing inside the mother's body, the baby is ready to be born. Other females look out for danger and help the young one to its feet after it is born.

Young elephants, called calves, are very hairy. This two-day-old calf is being supported by its mother's trunk. A calf's eyesight is poor, so the reassuring touch is important. Young elephants are cared for longer than any other mammals except humans.

8   A newborn elephant is able to walk a few hours after it is born. It already may weigh as much as 300 pounds (135 kilograms)! For the first few months, it will live on its mother's milk. Soon the baby elephant is ready to travel with the herd, watched closely by its mother and several "aunts."

When the calf is about six months old, it starts to eat vegetation in addition to milk. By putting its trunk into its mother's mouth, the calf can learn what she is eating. As it begins to find its own food, the calf starts exploring and playing with its cousins.

Young elephants are playful. They chase, push, and climb on one another. Calves play at fighting, learning the skills they will need in adult life. Playing also helps the calves form relationships with other elephants and learn their place in the family.

A young calf is the center of attention, and the slightest distress call brings its relatives running! By watching its elders carefully, the calf learns how to find its way during long journeys in search of food and water.

Elephants do not live in one place, but range over hundreds of square miles.

In the photograph, we see a herd moving through the bush. The herd often walks in single file, following traditional "elephant roads." Each family follows the matriarch, who remembers the best places for food and water during different seasons.

Elephants are vegetarians, and because they are so big they need more than 500 pounds (225 kilograms) of food each day. Their diet includes leaves, fruit, roots, and bark. They can even eat wood!

A trunk is a nose and an upper lip combined, but an elephant uses it like a hand. Trunks allow elephants to reach food high up in trees. A very young elephant may be able to reach the ground with its mouth, but older calves learn to pluck grass with their trunks.

Elephants also use their tusks to rip bark and dig up roots. Tusks are special ivory teeth. An elephant also has four molars. As these teeth are worn down, new sets grow from behind. When it is about 60 years old, the sixth and last set gets worn down. The elephant can no longer chew, and dies.

Elephants also like to drink at least once a day. When the family arrives at water, the oldest animals drink first and the calves must wait their turn. Elephants suck up water with their trunks. Then they put their trunks into their mouths and let the water flow down into their throats. It can take months for a calf to learn to use its trunk. Until then it drinks with its mouth.

Elephants are excellent swimmers and use their trunks like snorkels. Even the adults are playful and cool down by sinking into the water.

Elephants cool themselves in rivers or lakes, but they also avoid overheating by standing under trees. Calves rest in their mother's shadow. To prevent their skin from cracking, elephants roll in shallow water, covering themselves in a layer of mud. An elephant's skin can be up to 1¼ inches (3 centimeters) thick, but it is sensitive to insect bites. They scratch the itches against a tree.

Young elephants turn skin care into a game by spraying dust over each other. Life isn't all fun, though, and elephants must be aware of danger.

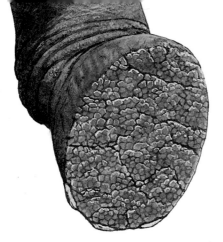

Elephants do not have many enemies. But lions kill young calves and humans can also be deadly. Elephants use their excellent senses of smell and hearing to explore their surroundings. If danger is detected, a group of elephants will immediately fall silent and bunch tightly around any calves. They may also retreat, and can run at up to 25 miles (40 kilometers) per hour over short distances. Surprisingly, elephants can move almost silently because of their cushioned feet. When the elephants stop, they sniff the air once more. If all is well, they relax, and the air is again full of contented rumblings.

Elephants communicate with each other all the time. They produce many different sounds: growls, snorts, trumpets, and screams, as well as deep stomach rumblings too low for humans to hear. Frightened elephants use their trunks to make spectacular trumpeting noises, and may flare out their ears to look bigger and more threatening. Communication helps to strengthen the bonds between group members, and is also important when different families meet.

Can you imagine the noise made when two elephant families meet? They come together with a lot of ear flapping and trumpeting. These elephants are greeting one another with the tips of their trunks, but others clash tusks or lean on each other. There are noisy reunions after even a short time apart!

All this excitement after a long journey makes the elephants sleepy. The calves roll onto their sides. The largest females stay standing when they sleep, with their heads hanging and their trunk tips resting on the ground. Now only the elephants' deep breathing can be heard.

Female elephants stay with the same family throughout their lives, unless the group gets too big. But males are often driven out when they are between 10 and 15 years old. Then they start to live on their own.

Bulls may live alone or in small, male-only groups. From time to time they search for a mate. They visit different families, trying to find a female that is ready to mate. Bulls rarely fight over cows. These bulls in the photograph are sparring to find out which is the stronger elephant.

Elephants usually live to be about 60 years old. Yet today the number of elephants is declining. They need vast areas to live in, but much of the land they once inhabited is now taken up by farms. Many elephants are protected in national parks, but in many places, poachers kill large numbers of elephants for their tusks, which are then used for ivory ornaments.

Elephants are the gentle giants of our world. We must find new ways to protect them so they will always be with us.

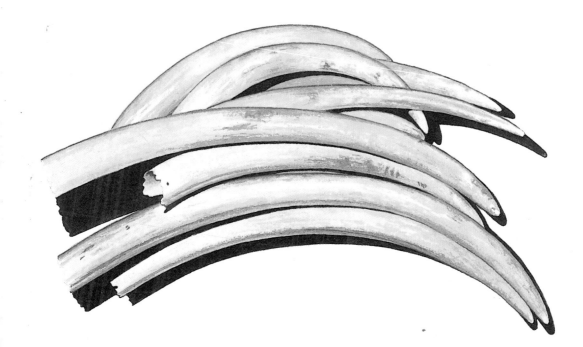

Fascinating facts

African

Elephants' ears are like radiators, letting out heat to help these enormous animals cool down.

Tusks grow throughout an elephant's life, but also get worn down by daily use. Just as we are left- or right-handed, elephants use one tusk more than the other, so one often becomes shorter.

Elephants are reluctant to leave dying relatives and are curious about the bones of others.

Asian elephants, which are smaller than African elephants, live in forests. Because forests are a cooler habitat, heat loss is not as important for them, so an Asian elephant's ears are also smaller.

Asian

African

Asian

Differences between African and Asian elephants:		
	African	**Asian**
Back	Dipped	Rounded
Ears	Big, cover shoulder	Smaller, do not cover shoulder
Forehead	Curved	Domed (sticks out)
Tusks	Long	Short (or absent, especially in females)
Trunk tip	Two lobes	Single lobe

Index